What C  ?

Written by Alex Adams
Illustrated by Cathy Johnson

Scott Foresman

What can we get
at the library?

We like books.

We get one, two, three books.

Vegetabl

Apples

Pears

What can we get
at the store?

We like apples.

We get one, two, three apples.

What can we get
at the pet shop?

We like fish.

We get one, two, three fish.

One, two, three.

One, two, three.

Look at what we have!